Originally published as *Think Big* in 2017 by Simple Truths, an imprint of Sourcebooks.

Photo Credits
Cover: Krista Kennell/Shutterstock, ASSOCIATED PRESS, colin powell/public domain, Jeff Bezos/Creative Commons 2.0
Internal: page vi, Monkey Business Images/Shutterstock; page 4, Gage Skidmore/WikiCommons; page 7, Krista Kennell/Shutterstock; page 9, Rob Kinmonth/Getty Images; page 13, Krista Kennell/Shutterstock; page 14, Matthew Yohe/WikiCommons; page 17, Hartsook/WikiCommons; page 20, Jean Meunier/Getty Images; page 23, Anton Gvozdikov/Shutterstock; page 26, Mass Communication Specialist 2nd Class Jordon Beesley/WikiCommons; page 28, Rawpixel.com/Shutterstock; page 32, Gage Skidmore/WikiCommons; page 35, Delivering Happiness Book/WikiCommons; page 37, WikiCommons; page 38, Steve Jurvetson/WikiCommons; page 41, Federal Reserve image/WikiCommons; page 42, ActuaLitté/WikiCommons; page 47, DoD News Features/WikiCommons; page 48, Allison Shirreffs/WikiCommons; page 51, Shawn Goldberg/Shutterstock; page 52, Joi Ito/WikiCommons; page 54, YP_Studio/Shutterstock; page 59, Harvard University/WikiCommons; page 60, WikiCommons; page 62, Time Life Pictures/Getty Images; page 65, WikiCommons; page 66, World Travel & Tourism Council/WikiCommons; page 69, Patriciahenritze/WikiCommons; page 71, USASOC News Service/WikiCommons; page 72, Levin Corbin Handy/WikiCommons; page 75, Lnobles/WikiCommons; page 76, Joi/WikiCommons; page 78, Paul C. Lasewicz/WikiCommons; page 80, Rawpixel.com/Shutterstock; WikiCommons; page 85, Joi/WikiCommons; page 87, Sterling.morris/WikiCommons; page 88, WikiCommons; page 91, mikeandryan/WikiCommons; page 92, World Economic Forum/WikiCommons; page 94, Marcel Antonisse & Anefo/WikiCommons; page 97, aradaphotography/Shutterstock; page 101, LizaKoz/WikiCommons; page 103, Alan Light/WikiCommons; page 104, David Shankbone/WikiCommons; page 106, Rawpixel.com/Shutterstock; page 110, USA International Trade Administration/WikiCommons; page 112, Frances Benjamin Johnston/WikiCommons; page 116, Tinseltown/Shutterstock; page 119, Northfoto/Shutterstock; page 121, Randy Miramontez/Shutterstock; page 122, Library of Congress/WikiCommons; page 125, Oracle Corporate Communications/WikiCommons; page 126, WikiCommons; page 128, The Library of Congress/WikiCommons; page 131, Håkan Dahlström/WikiCommons; page 132, Monkey Business Images/Shutterstock; page 137, Raimund Kommer/WikiCommons; page 139, mark reinstein/Shutterstock; page 141, Matt Becker/WikiCommons; page 142, Russell and Sons/WikiCommons; page 145, Mindy Kittay/WikiCommons; page 146, Eva Rinaldi/WikiCommons; page 148, Nobel Foundation/WikiCommons; page 151, WikiCommons; page 155, Cecil Stoughton/WikiCommons; page 156, WikiCommons; page 156, Bart Sherkow/Shutterstock; page 159, Hamilton83/WikiCommons; page 160, Cushing Memorial Library and Archives/WikiCommons; page 162, Rawpixel.com/Shutterstock; page 167, U.S. House of Representatives/WikiCommons; page 168, Yuliya Shauerman/Shutterstock; page 171, Black Board/WikiCommons; page 172, WikiCommons; page 175, Public Domain/WikiCommons; page 177, WikiCommons; page 181, Public Domain/WikiCommons; page 182, Knox Series/WikiCommons; page 184, Levin C. Handy/WikiCommons; page 187, Vern Evans/WikiCommons; page 188, Sarah Rozenthuler and Gil Dekel/WikiCommons; page 190, Flamingo Images/Shutterstock; page 194, Kingkongphoto/WikiCommons; page 197, NASA/WikiCommons; page 201, NBC Television/WikiCommons; page 202, Loadmaster David R. Tribble/WikiCommons; page 204, A.F. Bradley/WikiCommons; page 206, Roger Higgins/WikiCommons; page 211, Kingkongphoto/WikiCommons; page 213, NBC Radio and NBC Photo/WikiCommons; page 214, Loadmaster/WikiCommons.

Published by Simple Truths, an imprint of Sourcebooks
P.O. Box 4410, Naperville, Illinois 60567-4410
(630) 961-3900
sourcebooks.com

Printed and bound in China.

PP 10 9 8 7 6 5 4 3 2 1

CONTENTS

Introduction.. iv

Chapter 1: Pit Bull Management............................1

Chapter 2: You Just Don't Understand......................29

Chapter 3: The Unfair Advantage..........................55

Chapter 4: In Search of the Magic Bullet.................81

Chapter 5: How to Make Penguins Fly......................107

Chapter 6: Sliding Down the Razor Blade of Life..........133

Chapter 7: Slaying Life's Goliaths.......................163

Chapter 8: Let's Get Serious about Humor.................191

About the Author...216

INTRODUCTION

For more than thirty years, I've kept busy at meetings and conferences, jotting down the salient snippets shared by world-class speakers and entrepreneurs. My fascination with quotes started when I was an award-winning radio news editor, then a TV anchorman, and ultimately the editor-publisher of an issues and business weekly newspaper. I was recruited to become a part of an incredible business community called Vistage, eventually becoming their first chairman in the southeast.

Since my involvement with this international organization for company presidents and CEOs in 1987, I've heard more than one thousand world-class speaker presentations. Nearly one thousand opportunities to grab a sage bit of wisdom have presented themselves, resulting in a collection from the best and brightest minds across

industries. Each quote has the potential to affect the way you think about your business, the way you innovate and excel. I hope you enjoy this latest collection and continue to grow every time you open its pages.

CHAPTER 1

PIT BULL MANAGEMENT

Terse commentary providing laser-focused insight—how no-nonsense, bottom line— driven management behaves...or should.

By most standards, entrepreneurs drive our economy. The largest number of companies in our country are entrepreneurially owned, employing more than 70 percent of all workers, and have the most substantial bottom line.

As author Michael Gerber pointed out in his book *The E-Myth*, most entrepreneurial companies are started by someone with an idea for a product or a service. Started by the only people who aren't guaranteed a paycheck when they put the key in the lock each morning. High risk, hopefully for a high reward.

Gerber goes on to note that most successful entrepreneurs ultimately recognize their company has outgrown them and that they need professional management if the company is to continue to grow and profit. Enter the professional manager, someone with a formal education specifically designed for this sort of opportunity.

The guy with the great idea probably still employs most of the people with whom he started, including those the company outgrew long ago. The founder generally wants to make sure long-term employees (now called *team members*) share in the success when the company is sold. And, if he fits the stereotype, the entrepreneur is a world-class champion at conflict avoidance. He has never fired anyone too soon, and many far too late. One CEO with whom I worked made the same report to his Vistage peer group each month saying, "I successfully avoided firing Scott for another month."

The professional manager likely has a guaranteed contract, providing him more money than the entrepreneur has been taking and maybe a shot at equity. He certainly has a detailed plan providing structure, process, and accountability. His job is to study the key indicators and make educated decisions based on the numbers and indisputable facts, but not on personal feelings or relationships. The professional manager subscribes to management coach Bob Thomson's mantra that the best thing you can do for a good employee is to fire a bad one. That, in a nutshell, is focused, tenacious Pit Bull Management.

Never take advice from someone who doesn't have to live with the *consequences*.

—Mark Cuban, owner of the Dallas Mavericks

Most businesses rise or fall not because of the product, *but the people*.

—Steve Case, cofounder of America Online (AOL)

Bad decisions made with good intentions are *still bad decisions.*

—Jim Collins, business consultant, author

Don't cheat your people out of the *opportunity to win* because of your discomfort holding people accountable.

—Michael Canic, president of Bridgeway Leadership, Vistage speaker

---

If you don't make dust, you eat it.

—Bernie Marcus, cofounder and CEO of Home Depot

"

In looking for people to hire,
you look for three qualities:
integrity, intelligence, and energy.
And if they don't have the first,
the other two will kill you.

—Warren Buffett, chairman and CEO of Berkshire Hathaway

If you can't change the people, *change the people.*

—Michael Canic, president of Bridgeway Leadership, Vistage speaker

Conflict in most organizations is phony and designed to relieve people of having to take a risk and do anything significant.

—Jerry Harvey, PhD, professor at George Washington University, Vistage speaker

Recognize efforts; reward results.

—Catherine Meek, compensation expert, Vistage speaker

As it turns out, plants and dollars can be managed, but people expect leadership.

—D. Wayne Calloway, chairman and CEO of PepsiCo

Goals produce results, not activities.

—John McNeil, chief culture officer of Cancer Treatment Centers of America, Vistage speaker

If you haven't restructured your company in the past three years *you're in trouble.* **A company is not a Catholic marriage—forever.** *It's California style—one year at a time.*

—Ichak Adizes, PhD, founder and CEO of Adizes Institute

If you can't solve a problem, enlarge it.

—Dwight D. Eisenhower, U.S. president

The most expensive time in a manager's life is the time between when you truly lose faith in someone and when you do something about it.

—Jack Daly, professional sales coach, Vistage speaker

Trust your gut; don't cover your butt.
They pay you to do what is right.

—Paul Richards, professional baseball player

If your presence doesn't make an impact, your absence won't make a difference.

—Unknown

If we want to maintain the quality, the integrity, and the whole culture of our company, we've got to own it.

—S. Truett Cathy, founder of Chick-fil-A

Everyone has a plan—until he gets hit.

—Mike Tyson, professional boxer

Hire character. Train skill.

—Peter Schutz, president and CEO of Porsche, Vistage speaker

Done is better than perfect.

—Sheryl Sandberg, chief operating officer of Facebook, author

What kills a company is that stuff that is so quiet, so low profile, so off the screen that you never see it.

—Donald Phin, president of HRSherpas, Vistage speaker

13

It doesn't make sense to hire smart people and then tell them what to do; *we hire smart people so they can tell us what to do.*

—Steve Jobs, cofounder and CEO of Apple

Unhappy people attract other unhappy people, and in a small company that can *kill you.*

—Charlie King, founder of King Industrial Realty

The telling difference between companies in an industry is what they do when things go wrong.

—Bud Mingledorff, owner and chairman of Mingledorff's

Integrity matters.

—Andy Vabulas, founder and CEO of I.B.I.S.

You can't build a reputation on what you're *going to do.*

—Henry Ford, founder of Ford Motor Company

You don't want to be in a commodity business unless you're the *biggest, meanest kid on the block and* you have the lowest price.

—Jerry Goldress, chairman emeritus of GGG Partners, Vistage speaker

Excuses and results are *mutually exclusive.*

—Jim Bleech, CEO of Parliament Building Products, Vistage speaker

Too many companies let bad leaders hide behind good numbers.

—Richard Hadden, leadership consultant, Vistage Speaker

Good credit is for sissies.

—Vincent Forese, president and CEO of Link-Systems International

Every company eventually puts their ox in a ditch. That's when you go after their best people and customers, even if your ox is in the same ditch.

—Bud Mingledorff, owner and chairman of Mingledorff's

The janitor gets to explain why something went wrong. *Senior management does not.*

—Steve Jobs, cofounder and CEO of Apple

Intolerable performance exists when intolerable performance is tolerated.

—Dennis Snow, customer service consultant, Vistage Speaker

Leadership is one of the things you cannot delegate. You either exercise it or you *abdicate it.*

—Roberto Goizueta, chairman and CEO of The Coca-Cola Company

Not dead. Can't quit.

—Richard Machowicz, Navy SEAL veteran, TV host

If you think all your customers are created equally, you're headed for bankruptcy.

—Jim Cecil, cofounder and president of Nurture Marketing, Vistage speaker

Not harder, *smarter*.

—Matt Stoughton, president of BLS Enterprises

The reason marketing exists is to make it easier for sales to sell.

—Jeff Fisher, chief sales officer of I.B.I.S.

We've got so many problems that we can't help but solve some.

—David Hanson, founder and CEO of SyncroFlo

You are not your target market.

—Jim Cecil, cofounder and president of
Nurture Marketing, Vistage speaker

**At the end of the day, you bet on
people, not on strategies.**

—Lawrence Bossidy, CEO of AlliedSignal

**Accountability requires consequences.
You can't have one without the other.**

—Don Schmincke, president of Methods
International, Vistage speaker

Only the paranoid survive.

—Andy Grove, cofounder and CEO of Intel Corporation

The second you get an inkling somebody is not working out, *you're already late.*

—Jerry Goldress, chairman emeritus of GGG Partners, Vistage speaker

The best way to keep a good employee is to *fire a bad one.*

—Bob Thomson, management coach, Vistage speaker

Motivation is simple. You *eliminate those* who are not motivated.

—Lou Holtz, football coach

The conditions necessary to cause your largest client to disappear are in place and have been activated.

—Sam Bowers, consultant, Vistage speaker

When luck is your only backup strategy, it's really troubling.

—Clay Shirky, associate professor at New York University

It is not necessary to change. Survival is not mandatory.

—W. Edwards Deming, founder of the
W. Edwards Deming Institute

"Why" is not a word used by effective management.

—Charles Lipman, CEO of DiversiTech

27

CHAPTER 2

YOU JUST DON'T UNDERSTAND

Some things are obvious, but only from the other side of the desk.

David was the CEO of a company that manufactures pumping systems for high-rises and golf courses. As with most manufacturers, waste and "do over" work cost dollars that otherwise would have fallen to the bottom line. The guys on the floor just didn't understand.

It was end of the year, time for bonuses (a certificate for a Christmas turkey and a bonus tied to company profitability). Everyone—office staff, sales, engineering, manufacturing—gathered for their annual event, hands out, visions of big bucks dancing in their heads. Coming through the door, everyone spotted a couple of armed policemen standing on either end of a sheet-draped table.

What was that all about?

David handed out the certificates and the bonus checks individually, with a word or two for everyone as he went down the line. Once done, he stepped back, and with some drama, pulled the sheet from the table, revealing stacks and stacks and stacks of money.

"That, what is on that table," he explained, "is how much money we wasted this year on scrap and having to do jobs a second time. That's money that could have been part of your bonus check."

With that, he started at one end pushing the all the stacks of money, under the watchful eye of the two policemen, into a trash can at the end of the table.

Before, they just didn't understand. Now they did.

It's hard to *boss* your buddies.

—Leo Wells, chairman of Wells Real Estate Funds

Good customer service is not synonymous with masochism.

—Michael Hyatt, chairman and CEO of Thomas Nelson Publishers

31

Success unshared is failure.

—John Paul DeJoria, cofounder of Paul Mitchell Products

Managers promote stability while leaders press for change, and only organizations that embrace both sides of that contradiction can thrive in turbulent times.

—John Kotter, Harvard Business professor, author

It wasn't raining when Noah built the ark.

—Anonymous

When an idea is at your desk, it's yours; when it's up on the wall, it's everybody's.

—Tim Jones, director of strategy of 72andSunny

There's no such thing as a *sustainable advantage*; ask Kodak, Blockbuster, and BlackBerry.

—Michael Canic, president of Bridgeway Leadership, Vistage speaker

Your company's culture and your company's brand are really just two sides of the same coin.

Your culture is your brand.

—Tony Hsieh, CEO of Zappos

Winning alone is a sorry celebration.

—Rob Bellmar, EVP of business operations of West Unified Communications Services

A reputation is easier *kept than recovered.*

—Randy Fretz, chief of staff of Wells Real Estate Funds

You're not truly successful as a CEO until a client calls and you have no idea what he's talking about.

—Walt Kiser, CEO of Law Engineering

Never tell people how to do things. Tell them what to do, and they will surprise you with their ingenuity.

—General George Patton, U.S. Army

I am a leader; therefore, I must follow.

—Unknown

37

We see our customers as invited guests to a party, and we are the hosts. It's our job every day to make every important aspect of the customer experience *a little bit better.*

—Jeff Bezos, founder and CEO of Amazon.com

Agreement is a problem. Once we agree with others, *we have to share their risk*.

—Jerry Harvey, PhD, professor at George
Washington University, Vistage speaker

A great place to work is one where employees trust the people they work for, have pride in what they do, and enjoy the people they work with.

—Robert Levering, cofounder of the
Great Place to Work Institute

All selling is about *trust*.

—Duane Lakin, PhD, manager assessment specialist, Vistage speaker

If it is not in the interest of the public, it is not in the interest of business.

—Joseph H. Defrees, U.S. congressman

If it's a really big deal, your salespeople will screw it up.

—Tom Searcy, founder of Hunt Big Sales, Vistage speaker

Want to read your customer's mind? Too late. She just changed it.

—SAP.com ad

If I say something which you understand fully in this regard, I probably made a mistake.

—Alan Greenspan, chairman of the U.S. Federal Reserve

No executive has ever suffered because his subordinates were strong and effective.

—Peter Drucker, professor at Claremont Graduate University

41

Potential has a shelf life.

—Margaret Atwood, author and essayist

Whenever you see a successful business, someone once made a courageous decision.

—Peter Drucker, professor at Claremont Graduate University

People can't see it your way until you first see it their way.

—Jack Kaine, management consultant, Vistage speaker

The man who says he is willing to meet you halfway is usually *a poor judge of distance.*

—Laurence J. Peter, author

Being a customer is voluntary.

—Charles E. Foster, manager of Alexander Lumber Company

You don't own your customers— you lease them, and sometimes for only a very short time.

—Bernie Marcus, cofounder and CEO of Home Depot

Profit is the applause you get from appreciative customers and committed employees.

—Ken Blanchard, author

Your customer will take the word of a customer service rep over that of a salesman.

—Chuck Reaves, sales trainer, Vistage speaker

Most people don't need a boss; they need someone to listen to them.

—Maurice Mascarenhas, Vistage speaker

People remember people who remember them.

—Marshall Field, founder of Marshall Field and Company

Perpetual optimism is a force multiplier.

—General Colin Powell, U.S. secretary of state

Communication is not a two-way street; nobody has to listen.

—Bill Graham, cofounder and CEO of Facility Solutions Group, Vistage speaker

47

A relationship is not something that you pursue; it's what happens to you when you are immersed in serving the dreams of your customer.

—Tom Peters, author

People are the only sustainable advantage of an organization.

—Richard Teerlink, chairman and CEO of Harley-Davidson

Lower your price enough, and your better customers will leave you.

—Chuck Reaves, sales trainer, Vistage speaker

Consumers today are often better informed than the salesmen themselves.

—Marcus Sheridan, co-owner of The Sales Lion, Vistage speaker

A customer's desire to be treated with respect and have their business *appreciated* is the only "fixed" in the variable world of business.

—Clark Johnson, chairman and CEO of Pier 1 Imports, Vistage speaker

People rarely buy what they need. They buy what they want.

—Seth Godin,
entrepreneur, marketer

The purpose of getting our folks to join organizations is not to get them to know everybody; *it's to get everybody to know them.*

—Charlie King, owner of King Industrial Realty

When two men always agree, one of them is unnecessary.

—William Wrigley Jr., founder of Wrigley

We do not see things as they are; we see things as we are.

—Anonymous

A bonus is a gift. People have no idea how or why they got it.

—Kent Romanoff, management consultant, Vistage speaker

53

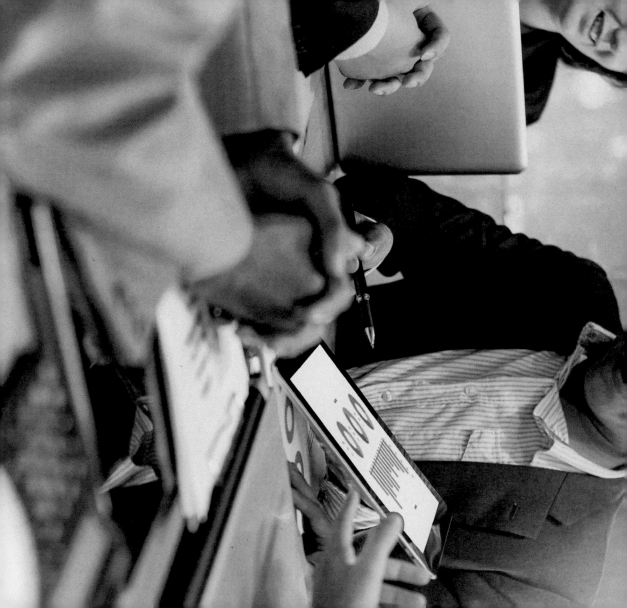

CHAPTER 3

THE UNFAIR ADVANTAGE

Every viable product or service has an "unfair advantage" over its competition. What's yours?

C had had been running a start-up company for several years. After doing well as a professional manager, he'd made the difficult transition from hired gun to entrepreneur. The company was all his—his and the bank's.

His Vistage advisory group had become concerned that as the company grew, it might be outgrowing some of its people. Chad was loyal—to a fault, his colleagues thought. The group had listened to a speaker who told them it wasn't a question of if, but of when a company outgrows its people. In Chad's case, the advisory group questioned his controller's continued employment.

Chad explained that his guy had been with him since day one. He had the numbers on Chad's desk each month within ten business days; he kept accurate financial records, reconciled the bank statements, and did a great job of making sure that not only were invoices being paid, but also that discounts were being taken.

"No longer enough. Should be getting more," group members challenged. "Consider making a larger investment (Chad saw it as overhead) and upgrade to a different controller."

Ultimately, with oft-stated misgivings, he did.

The lesson learned, quoting a source we've never been able to identify, was: "If your company were a ship, a good CFO would be in the bow charting the course, not on the stern recording the wake." Chad's top man in finance had done a great job of telling him what had happened, but had never considered moving to the front of the boat and looking at what was, or could be, next.

With a new occupant, the office next to the CEO's was soon providing a whole new palette of financial services. Trailing twelve-month charts took the seasonality out of the numbers. Lines of credit were more easily negotiated by someone who spoke bank talk. The new financial management guy managed cash flow, understood risk management, and likely most importantly, became integral to all the company's financial and strategic long-term planning. Upgrading his top man in finance proved to be an investment for which Chad was getting a great return. And an unfair advantage.

It's always good when followers believe in their leaders, but it's even better when leaders believe in their followers.

—Mardy Grothe, PhD, psychologist, author, Vistage speaker

Most people stay mediocre to protect against loss.

—Morrie Shechtman, chairman of Fifth Wave Leadership, Vistage speaker

Consider the postage stamp: its usefulness consists in the ability to stick to one thing until it gets there.

—Josh Billings, humorist

Judge a man by his questions rather than his answers.

—Voltaire, philosopher

59

Anyone who stops learning is old, whether at twenty or eighty. Anyone who keeps *learning stays young*. The greatest thing in life is to keep your mind young.

—Henry Ford, founder of Ford Motor Company

In a time of drastic change, it is the learner who will *inherit* the future.

—Eric Hoffer, philosopher

Good marketing makes the company look smart. Great marketing makes the customer feel smart.

—Joe Chernov, VP of Marketing of InsightSquared

Most people are much better at waiting to speak than listening.

—Steve Wiley, president of the Lincoln Leadership Institute, Vistage speaker

Leaders describe the future, compelling and with clarity.

—Dan Barnett, owner and CEO of the Primavera Company, Vistage speaker

Culture is the last remaining opportunity to separate yourself in a commoditized world.

—David Friedman, author, Vistage speaker

Risk more than others think is safe. *Dream more than others think is practical.*

—Anonymous

What we need is less process and more passion.

—Frank Maguire, senior VP of KFC, Vistage speaker

If you want to be *Superman*, you've got to learn to fly in bad weather.

—Michael Canic, president of Bridgeway Leadership, Vistage speaker

Every now and then, a man's mind is stretched *by a new idea or sensation and* never shrinks *back to its former dimensions.*

—Oliver Wendell Holmes Sr, physician, poet

It's more important to *hire* people with the *right qualities* than with the right experience.

—J. W. Marriott, founder of the Marriott Corporation

Make sure that bad news travels quickly to those who can do something about it.

—Michael LeBoeuf, author

Nothing gives one person so much advantage over another as to *remain cool and unruffled under all circumstances.*

—Thomas Jefferson, U.S. president

If you can't make decisions and build relationships, you won't have a job in the future.

—Morrie Shechtman, chairman of Fifth Wave Leadership, Vistage speaker

Every time you fail, you get a piece of the answer as to *how to succeed.*

—Derreck Kayongo, CEO of the National Center for Civil and Human Rights, Vistage speaker

The definition of knowledge has changed. Knowledge used to mean knowing how to do something. Now it means *knowing where to go to get something done.*

—Dick Gorelick, president of Gorelick & Associates

Your attitude controls your destiny—in business as well as in health.

—Jerry Kornfield, MD, family physician, Vistage speaker

My first message is: Listen; listen, listen to the people who do the work.

—H. Ross Perot, founder of Electronic Data Systems and Perot Systems

You'll never have all the information you need to make a decision. If you did, it would be a foregone conclusion, not a decision.

—David J. Mahoney, author

71

Discipline is the training that makes punishment unnecessary.

—Robert E. Lee, Confederate Army general

The new source of power is not money in the hands of the few, but information in the hands of many.

—John Naisbitt, author

Learning is the only sustainable source of competitive advantage.

—Karl Hellman, associate professor at Principia College, Vistage speaker

If you find yourself in a fair fight, you didn't plan your mission properly.

—Col. David Hackworth, U.S. Army

Under promise; over deliver.

—Tom Peters, author

The prize goes to the person who sees the future the quickest.

—William Stiritz, president of Westgate Equity Partners

Success is going from failure to failure *without loss of enthusiasm.*

—Anonymous

The key is not the will to win… **everybody has that. It is the will to** *prepare to win that is important.*

—Bobby Knight, college basketball coach

Commitment is essential in business. If you don't have it, you won't have any business.

—Michael Hyatt, chairman and CEO of Thomas Nelson Publishers

You can't stop learning. You have to continue to change and adapt.

—Joi Ito, director of MIT Media Lab

The way to succeed is to double your failure rate.

—Thomas Watson, chairman and CEO of IBM

In business the competition will bite you if you keep running; if you stand still, they will swallow you.

—William S. Knudsen, president of General Motors

The art and science of asking questions is the source of all knowledge.

—Thomas Berger, author

An investment in knowledge pays the best interest.

—Benjamin Franklin, founding father

Skills and savvy get you to the top, but *character's* what keeps you there.

—Rick Goings, chairman and CEO of Tupperware Brands

79

CHAPTER 4

IN SEARCH OF THE MAGIC BULLET

The tough answer is that there are no easy answers. There are no magic bullets.

M att worked his way up in the business, ultimately buying out the current owners and attaching his manufacturing-distribution company to a rocket. His monthly report to his peer advisory group nearly always included an acquisition and increased sales. Focusing on Values (he capitalized the word), building a strong culture, and maintaining an unswerving commitment to quality, the company soon topped one hundred million, then two…and was on its way to three when the news came.

The new owner, the guy who took so much pride in the jobs he was creating, the markets he was opening, the changes he was effecting, was diagnosed with an illness that could only get worse. And stress had accelerated the deterioration of his health.

He'd been the target of others when the company was smaller. Now, in search of an exit that would let him retire to focus on his health and his rapidly growing art collection, Matt decided to take the company public. His plan was to turn the reins over to a professional manager, a new CEO. An IPO would open the door for his exit. That would be his magic bullet.

One problem: Matt was a very private guy who found it difficult to share the numbers. Each exec within the company knew how they were doing, but not the specifics of how the company was doing overall. Be that as it may, investment bankers put a book together, and Matt began what was planned to be a long series of road shows designed to whet the appetite for stock when the company went public.

Only it didn't.

Meeting with him at his office, I asked a question: "Matt, how are you going to handle monthly calls from a thirty-five-year-old analyst demanding to know why you're not providing unending quarters of ever-increasing profitability?" There was silence and then resignation that maybe his good idea really wasn't.

Matt made three calls, reaching Warren Buffett the third time. Buffett flew into town over the weekend and told Matt he "liked buying companies from owners who took pride and were enthusiastic about their companies." They shook hands on a Saturday and had the lawyers working on details Monday.

Matt's search for a magic bullet came to an end when he picked up the telephone on the corner of his desk and made three calls.

Passion for who you are and what you do will carry you a lot further than just knowledge!

—Bob Dabic, Vistage group chairman

The secret to creativity is the art of hiding your sources.

—Anonymous

Simplify your message, and repeat often.

—John Lilly, partner with Greylock Partners

I want to stay as close to the edge as I can without going over. Out on the edge, you see all kinds of things you can't see from the center.

—Kurt Vonnegut, author

Without vision, we have no context for feedback; we're just responding to what someone else values or wants.

—Stephen R. Covey, author

Patience, persistence, and perspiration make an unbeatable combination for success.

—Napoleon Hill, author

A comfort zone is a beautiful place, but nothing grows there.

—Unknown

Leaders are visionaries with a poorly defined view of failure.

—Michael Siegel, entertainer

Being present has nothing to do with *where your feet are.*

—Chalmers Brothers, management consultant, author, Vistage speaker

We are drowning in information and starved for knowledge.

—John Naisbitt, author

Almost all big mistakes are made when people perceive things are going well.

—Jason Beans, founder and CEO of Rising Medical Solutions

A certain amount of opposition is a great help; *kites rise against, not with, the wind.*

—John Neal, author

A key driver for *relationships, revenue, and results is simplicity.*

—Jeff Blackman, owner of Blackman & Associates, Vistage speaker

Ideas are a commodity. **Execution of them is not.**

—Michael Dell, founder and CEO of Dell Technologies

There is no such thing as insufficient resources, only *insufficient resourcefulness.*

—Tony Hsieh, CEO of Zappos

91

Be a sponge.
Curiosity is life.
Assumption
is death.
Look around.

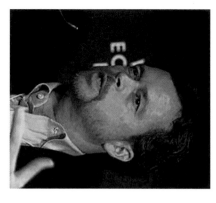

—Mark Parker, chairman and CEO of Nike

People invest in who you are and what you can do for them. One without the other only assures short-term success.

—Jeff Blackman, owner of Blackman & Associates, Vistage speaker

Transformation is never done; *continuous evolution is critical.*

—Victor Luis, CEO of Coach

People in distress will sometimes *prefer a problem that is familiar to a solution that is not.*

—Neil Postman, professor at New York University, author

A mistake happens only once; *underperformance is a pattern.*

—Greg Bustin, president of Bustin & Co., Vistage speaker

If you're not having fun, there's no passion. If there's no passion, there can be *no success*.

—Peter Schutz, president and CEO of Porsche, *Vistage* speaker

New? New is easy. Right is hard.

—Craig Federighi, senior VP of software engineering of Apple

Leadership is about taking the organization to a place it would not have otherwise gone without you, in a value-adding, measurable way.

—George M. C. Fisher, chairman and CEO of Motorola

The quality of your questions determines the quality of your life.

—Lee Milteer, author

Mere change is not growth. Growth is the synthesis of change and continuity, and where there is no continuity, there is no growth.

—C. S. Lewis, author

In times of rapid change, experience may be your own worst enemy.

—J. Paul Getty, founder of the Getty Oil Company

Everything should be made as simple as possible and no simpler.

—Unknown

Spoon-feeding in the long run teaches us nothing but the shape of the spoon.

—E. M. Forster, author

If you have an opportunity to *grow your company* and you really believe in it, the capital will follow you.

—Gordon Tunstall, founder and president of Tunstall Consulting, Vistage speaker

The best ideas for *improving a job* come from those who do it every day.

—Jim Bleech, CEO of Parliament Building Products, Vistage speaker

The greatest difficulty lies not in persuading people to *accept* new ideas but in persuading them to *abandon* old ones.

—John Maynard Keynes, economist

Never have a strategic partner with *values different from yours.*

—Jerry Goldress, chairman emeritus of GGG Partners, Vistage speaker

I believe that *you should praise people whenever you can; it causes* **them to respond as a thirsty plant responds to water.**

—Mary Kay Ash, founder of Mary Kay Cosmetics

66

Sometimes I think I understand everything—then I regain consciousness.

—Ray Bradbury, author

99

If you don't provide opportunities to grow, people leave.

—Tom Colicchio, founder of Crafted Hospitality

Eagles don't flock. You have to find them one at a time.

—H. Ross Perot, founder of Electronic Data Systems and Perot Systems

Your business success depends on focusing on *the things to come*— not the things that were.

—Carlos Rizowy, author, Vistage speaker

Every problem in business has *already been solved.*

—Robert Stephens, founder of the Geek Squad

Sometimes the truth depends on *a walk around the lake.*

—Wallace Stevens, poet

105

CHAPTER 5

HOW TO MAKE PENGUINS FLY

Brief explanations of how to accomplish the seemingly impossible.

I f the conflict avoiders of the world hosted a competition, my money would have been on Mark. He had faith—blind, unyielding faith—that if he worked just a little longer, he could make his penguins fly.

They were a ragtag group of executives that Mark insisted were part of a team, and despite glaring issues, they performed that way—at least most of them did.

When the executives updated each other during Vistage peer advisory meetings, Mark was not shy about discussing the issues he was having with his manufacturing manager in Texas. The group finally pushed him into sharing the full details in executive session and then unanimously (a rarity in any room with sixteen CEOs) said he needed to fire Scott.

Mark explained that Scott had been with them for years. Perhaps if he had a little more time, maybe attended a few seminars, he would come around. Then started a ritual memorialized in anecdotal form.

For literally twelve months, Mark started each of his monthly updates with the same phrase: "I successfully avoided firing Scott for another month."

Poked and prodded by his contemporaries, Mark finally pulled the trigger and replaced Scott with an all-star—an eagle who, if you will, soared where there had only been a penguin that couldn't fly.

You can't make a good deal with a bad person.

—Warren Buffett, chairman and CEO of Berkshire Hathaway

Those having torches will pass them on to others.

—Plato, philosopher

Bloom where you're planted.

—Anonymous

Let your marginal employee work *across the street.*

—Eric Coryell, founder of Core Connections, *Vistage speaker*

Take people out of the organization the *same way you brought them in*—with respect.

—Ann Rhoades, VP of HR of Wilmington Trust, *Vistage speaker*

An expert is one who knows more *and more about less and less.*

—Nicholas Murray Butler, president of Columbia University

Few things can help an individual more than to place responsibility on him and to let *him know that you trust him.*

—Booker T. Washington, educator, author

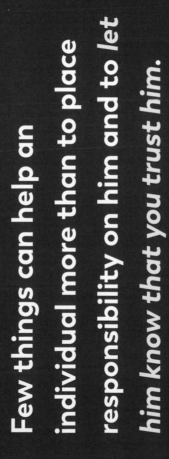

Important and relevant are *not the same thing.*

—Brad Remillard, founding partner of IMPACT Hiring Solutions, Vistage Speaker

Really good employees choose to do more than "just enough."

—Jay Forte, founder of the Greatness Zone, Vistage speaker

You have to *leave the safety of the sidewalk* to get to the other side of the street.

—Don Cottle, management consultant, Vistage group chairman

The world makes way for the man who knows where he is going.

—Ralph Waldo Emerson, poet

Be careful how you *spend* your people.

—Rick Detienne, president of Laminations

Holding people accountable *who have no sense of ownership* is simply imposing upon people.

—Mark Aesch, founder and CEO of TransPro, Vistage speaker

You are far too smart to be the only thing standing in your way.

—Jennifer Freeman, actress

You don't want to be considered just the best at what you do. You want to be known as the only one who does what you do.

—Bill Graham, concert promoter

Culture follows the leader.

—David Friedman, author, Vistage speaker

If you listen carefully, *very carefully*, people will tell you where they're going, what they're willing to do. *Don't assume.*

—Steve Harty, president and CEO of Greater Green Bay YMCA

If all possible objections must first be overcome, *nothing significant* will happen.

—Samuel Johnson, poet, writer

Strategy is a commodity; implementation is an art.

—Peter Drucker, professor at Claremont Graduate University

I much prefer people who *rock the boat* to people who jump out.

—Orson Welles, actor, director, filmmaker

The only thing *not replicable* worldwide is your people.

—Morrie Shechtman, chairman of Fifth Wave Leadership, Vistage speaker

Somebody has to do something, and it's *incredibly pathetic* that it has to be us.

—Jerry Garcia, singer/songwriter, the Grateful Dead

Given a reasonable opportunity, *the people at the bottom* will make a disproportionate contribution to *the success of your company.*

—Richard Palmer, cofounder of Triplejump, Vistage speaker

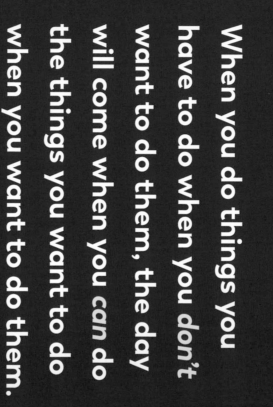

When you do things you have to do when you don't want to do them, the day will come when you *can* do the things you want to do when you want to do them.

—Zig Ziglar, motivational speaker, author

People may doubt what you say, but they will believe what you do.

—Lewis Cass, U.S. cabinet member

Success is not determined by *flawless* execution of a plan. It is determined by *how people react to failure*.

—Don Schmincke, president of Methods International, Vistage speaker

Nothing is impossible for the man who doesn't have to do it himself.

—A. H. Weiler, *New York Times* film critic

It's never too late to be what you might have been.

—Unknown

When you have a choice to make and don't make it, that, in itself, *is a choice.*

—William James, philosopher

Results are ancient history; how are you managing the future?

—Dan Barnett, owner and CEO of the Primavera Company, Vistage speaker

The *new guy* learns from the *old guy* who learned from the *dead guy*.

—Scott Stratman, consultant

Management is about coping with complexity. Leadership is about coping with change.

—John Kotter, Harvard business professor, author

I had all the *disadvantages required for* success.

—Larry Ellison, cofounder and CEO of Oracle

Your company's best ideas are not born by stressed people staring at a computer at work.

—Diana Martinez, CEO of SPARK! Creative Consulting, Vistage speaker

125

Visibility is credibility.

—Kate Cole, group president of Focus Brands, COO of Cinnabon

The highest reward for a person's toil is *not what they get for it but what they become by it.*

—John Ruskin, art critic

If you only give people what they already want, someone else will give them what they never dreamed possible.

—Unknown

Faced with the choice between changing one's mind and proving that there is no need to do so, almost everybody gets busy on the proof.

—John Kenneth Galbraith, professor at Harvard University, author

You take people as far as they will go, not as far as you would like them to go.

—Jeannette Rankin, U.S. Congresswoman

I can argue with the way you think; but I can't argue with the way you feel.

—Mikki Williams, CEO of Mikki Williams Unltd, Vistage speaker

See everything, overlook a great deal, and correct a little.

—Pope John XXIII

Learn to say *no* and it will be of more use to you than to be able to read Latin.

—Charles Haddon Spurgeon, Baptist preacher

You miss 100 percent of the shots you don't take.

—Wayne Gretzky, professional hockey player, coach

Every single human *becomes great* when they set goals that inspire their heart and soul.

—Roxanne Emmerich, CEO of the Emmerich Group, author

CHAPTER 6

SLIDING DOWN THE RAZOR BLADE OF LIFE

A key phrase from one of satirist Tom Lehrer's songs evokes the pain of inevitable truths.

L ynn Anderson sold millions of records reminding folks no one promises anyone a rose garden. Sometimes a made-for-each-other romance can end up on the rocks.

Walt had started as a professional manager in a financial services company and grew in rank and responsibility as the company expanded—until it hit a bad patch and rapidly plummeted to the point that bankruptcy was all but inevitable. Eager to avoid the stigma of having one of their companies go bankrupt, the folks at headquarters offered Walt the whole mess for a dollar. He agreed, with the provision that he also be given the money set aside to settle a spate of lawsuits.

The troops rallied, and Walt brought the company back from the brink. He was good at negotiating and started making money, profiting on the funds that had been set aside to settle pending litigation. Those funds were then used for hiring good talent and expanding services.

Life was good; Walt adapted to new technology and came up with a service that made it difficult for clients to leave. More and more black ink settled on the bottom line. Then the calls started. Was he, could he be, interested in selling? Having sold slices of ownership to his management team, he felt an obligation to listen, and as the numbers started coming in, it became obvious that he needed to sell if he was going to provide liquidity for the people who had worked with him to create this great success.

It came down to two companies: one was offering $49 a share, the other $53. The first was a company Walt knew well. They pledged to keep his team, offering him a contract, and had a culture that aligned closely with Walt's company's. The second was a by-the-numbers operation that thought people were largely expendable. They wanted Walt to stay through the transition, but that would be it. Their reputation was of having only one focus: the bottom line.

How much was enough? Walt told his Vistage advisory group

that he was going to get a check for more than he ever could have imagined, and while he could then retire, his key execs likely would not, so he opted for less ($49 per share)—figuring that the money was more than enough and his goals of providing for his team and assuring their future were being met. And he'd stay on to help take the company to a new level.

Two years later, the company that finished second bought the company that finished first. Things changed, Walt's assumptions about that company proved correct, and he left. As satirist Tom Lehrer so graphically put it, Walt had taken "a slide down the razor blade of life."

That rose had thorns.

If you have everything under control, you're not going fast enough.

—Mario Andretti, race car driver

The measure of success is not whether you have a tough problem to deal with but whether it is the *same problem you had last year.*

—John Foster Dulles, U.S. secretary of state

137

When things are bad, we take comfort in the thought that they could always get worse. And when they are, we find hope in the thought that things are so bad they have to get better.

—Malcolm Forbes, chairman and publisher of *Forbes* magazine

Anyone not pulling his weight is probably pushing his luck.

—Randy Fretz, chief of staff of Wells Real Estate Funds

You have to have *purpose*, you have to have *vision*, and most importantly, you must share it with the people in your organization.

—Dr. Gerald Faust, founder of Courseware

One lifetime isn't enough. Just when you start to learn, *it's time to go.*

—Luis Marden, *National Geographic* photographer and writer

If you choose not to decide, you have still *made a choice.*

—Geddy Lee,
singer/songwriter, Rush

The world's fastest strategic planning session: Where are you? *Where would you like to be?* How would you like to get there?

—Jeff Blackman, owner of Blackman &
Associates, Vistage speaker

141

We must take change by the hand, or rest assuredly, change will take us by the throat.

—Winston Churchill, prime minister of Great Britain

In God we trust; all others must bring data.

—W. Edwards Deming, founder of the
W. Edwards Deming Institute

Partnerships are not made in the womb.

—Bud Mingledorff, owner and chairman of Mingledorff's

Most companies grow themselves out of business; they either can't finance it or they can't manage it.

—Dr. Gerald Faust, founder of Courseware

If you're not living on the edge, you're taking up too much space.

—Tom Feltenstein, SVP of Bozell Advertising, Vistage speaker

You can't make a good decision with *bad information.*

—Kevin Schmuggerow, regional manager of HEPACO

In a bullfight, the bull perceives the cape as the problem, but it is the sword that kills him. *Are you chasing the cape or the sword?*

—Mike Bell, technical services leader of
ADP, Vistage group chairman

If we don't change our direction, we're likely to end up *where we're headed.*

—Chinese proverb

The truth will set you free, but first it will *piss you off.*

—Gloria Steinem, feminist, social activist

You must have *long-range goals* to keep from being frustrated by *short-term failures.*

—Charles C. Noble, author

When it's over—*no regrets.*

—Randall Peeters, PhD, aerospace chief scientist, Vistage speaker

Don't get so busy making a living that you forget to make a life.

—Dolly Parton, singer/songwriter

The only way I can tell that a *new idea is really important is the feeling of terror that seizes me.*

—James Franck, Nobel Prize–winning physicist

The longer it takes to close a deal, the less likely it is to happen; *time kills deals.*

—Marisa Pensa, CEO of Methods in Motion, Vistage speaker

148

There is more right with us than wrong with us, regardless how wrong we think we are.

—Jon Kabat-Zinn, PhD, founder of the Stress Reduction Clinic at University of Massachusetts

A smart man knows how to grow a company; a brilliant man knows when to sell it.

—Jeff McCart, CEO of the McCart Group

If your horse dies, get off.

—Sign in Kentucky field

Obstacles are those *frightful* things you see when you take your eyes off the goal.

—Anonymous

My interest is in the *future* because I am going to spend *the rest of my life there.*

—Charles F. Kettering, inventor, founder of Delco Electronics

Following the path of *least resistance is what makes rivers and men crooked.*

—Unknown

You just can't beat the person who won't give up.

—Babe Ruth, pro baseball player

Money in business is like gas in your car. You need to pay attention so you don't end up on the side of the road. But your trip is not a tour of gas stations.

—Tim O'Reilly, O'Reilly Media

Just think how happy you would be if you lost everything you have right now, and then got it back again.

—Frances Rodman, author

If you are not careful, your success in the past will block your chances to succeed in the future.

—Joel A. Barker, author, filmmaker

Emotion in a negotiation is *tantamount* to giving a loaded pistol to a monkey.

—Tom Parker, senior VP of Yukon, Vistage group chairman

Even if I knew that *tomorrow the world would go to pieces*, I would still *plant my apple tree*.

—Martin Luther, philosopher, theologian

The fear of loss is *twice the motivator* as the desire for gain.

—Dean Minuto, sales strategy and training coach, Vistage speaker

We enjoy the comfort of opinion without the discomfort of thought.

—John F. Kennedy, U.S. president

The man who views the world at *fifty* the same he did at twenty has wasted *thirty* years of his life.

—Mohammad Ali, heavyweight champion boxer

"Yes but" is "no" in a tuxedo.

—Diana Martinez, CEO of SPARK!
Creative Consulting, Vistage speaker

Nobody succeeds beyond his or her wildest expectations unless he or she begins with some wild expectations.

—Ralph Charell, author

No organization can make good decisions without conflict.

—Ian MacDougall, founder of Corporate LifeCycles, Vistage speaker

No one can guess the future loss of business from a dissatisfied customer.

—W. Edwards Deming, founder of the W. Edwards Deming Institute

Near-death experiences are very healthy for companies.

—David Cole, chairman of the Center for Automotive Research

Show me someone who has done something worthwhile, and I'll show you someone who has overcome adversity.

—Lou Holtz, college football coach

Happiness comes from moving toward getting what you want, *not from getting it.*

—Steven Snyder, founder of Snyder Leadership Group, Vistage speaker

I am convinced that if the *rate of change* inside an organization is less than the rate of change

outside, *the end is in sight.*

—Jack Welch, chairman and CEO of General Electric

159

I don't care to be involved in the crash landing unless I can be in on the takeoff.

—Harold Stassen, governor of Minnesota

Most see what is before them; the strategic leaders sense what is around the corner.

—Kirby Martzall, founder and CEO of KL Martzall, Vistage group chairman

If there's no such thing as *risk of loss*, there is no potential for *gain.*

—Leo Wells, chairman of Wells Real Estate Funds

The *way we see the problem* is the problem.

—Stephen R. Covey, author

How come every time I get *stabbed in the back, my fingerprints* are on the knife?

—Jerry Harvey, PhD, professor at George Washington University, Vistage speaker

161

CHAPTER 7

SLAYING LIFE'S GOLIATHS

A few pebbles for your business's slingshot.

Sometimes the little guy wins one. David did it with a slingshot, and Jim did it with a set of keys. They both slew Goliath.

Years before, Jim had invested in and then later took over running a company in one of the most basic areas of manufacturing. But when the economy turned soft, business predictably slowed, and profitability was evasive. A much larger competitor had expressed interest in buying the company. A few weeks into the early talks, a new and very big problem surfaced. The Occupational Safety and Health Administration had found that the small plot of land Jim's company sat on was contaminated. That hadn't been a factor (or had slipped by due diligence) when Jim's group bought the company. Remediation could cost a small fortune.

Making matters worse, the company was well into its five–million–dollar line of credit with the Big Bank up North; the potential buyer appeared to be scared off by the OSHA findings; and with no profit from the company for the last quarter, the bank was calling its line. What to do?

The Vistage advisory group went from shades of dark gray to gloomy black. A peripheral player having problems making money in a declining industry now found itself sitting on contaminated land, with heartless bankers a thousand miles away wanting their money back.

Close the doors and take Chapter 11 bankruptcy was the consensus among Jim's peers. Then one wizened professional manager suggested that Jim "give it back to them. You don't have the money. It's over. Give the bank the keys."

Turns out they didn't want the keys. The bank decided that five million was a small price to pay compared to the unknown cost of soil remediation, never mind the likelihood of finding someone eager to buy.

The bank tore up the note, telling Jim to keep the keys and the company. David felled Goliath with a well-aimed rock and a slingshot; Jim won his battle by tossing the keys on the desk.

Seven-foot-one former basketball star Wilt Chamberlain may have put it best when he said, "Nobody roots for Goliath."

—Lee Thayer, cofounder of the Thayer Institute, Vistage speaker

People tend to choose problems they cannot solve rather than make the choices or decisions they need to make.

The worst thing about fear is the fear it's going to get worse.

—Steven Snyder, founder of Snyder Leadership Group, Vistage speaker

The CEO's job is to get 100% out of everybody, and everybody is 100% different.

—Tim Ryan, U.S. chairman of PricewaterhouseCoopers

What would you attempt to do if you knew you could not fail?

—Unknown

"I've found that luck is quite predictable. If you want more luck, take more chances. Be more active. Show up more often.

—Brian Tracy, author

We live in an *informational society, but information is not knowledge and knowledge is not wisdom.*

—Ken Ruscio, emeritus professor of politics at Washington and Lee University

Unless you walk out into the unknown, the odds of making a profound difference in your life are pretty low.

—Tom Peters, Author

You have to have a dream so you can get up in the morning.

—Billy Wilder, filmmaker

Change in the marketplace *isn't* something to *fear*; it's an opportunity for you to *shuffle the deck.*

—Jack Welch, chairman and CEO of General Electric

The wise man draws more advantage from his enemies than a fool from his _friends_.

—Thomas Fuller, author

You have to do what you need to do before you can do what you want to do.

—Holly Middleton, PhD, psychologist, Vistage speaker

You can always see what goes wrong, but you can't see the cause. Causes are invisible.

—Bill Schwarz, author, Vistage speaker

The best way to resolve a problem in business is to address it before you're asked.

—Marcus Sheridan, co-owner of The Sales Lion, Vistage speaker

The company with the *best information wins* all the time.

—Pat Price, editor and game designer

You're not good at doing anything you only do once.

—Scott Steiding, VP of Morrison Hershfield

Most people *tiptoe through life* hoping they make it *safely to death.*

—Earl Nightingale, radio personality, author

We ask people to change *without showing them* what they can become.

—Sheila Sheinberg, founder of the Center for Life Cycle Sciences, Vistage speaker

There is only one thing more painful than learning from experience, and that is not learning from experience.

—Archibald MacLeish, poet, author

You are either *the leader or you are led.*

—Carlos Rizowy, author, Vistage speaker

Values are like fingerprints—
nobody's are the same,
but you leave 'em all over
everything you do.

—Elvis Presley, singer, actor

I've developed a new philosophy…I only dread one day at a time.

—Charlie Brown, character in *Peanuts* comic

Regret and fear are twin thieves who rob us of today.

—Robert J. Hastings, editor, author

If you can see the path in front of you laid out step by step, *then it's not your path*.

—Joseph Campbell, author

Life isn't about waiting for the storm to pass. It's about learning to dance in the rain.

—Unknown

People work *harder, longer, and better* if they believe their work is *meaningful and positive.*

—Rick Richard, chairman and CEO of Columbia Energy Group

Revenue is the measure of how hard we worked; *profit tells whether it was worth it.*

—John McKenney, CEO of McKenney's

Power is always dangerous. Power attracts the worst and corrupts the best.

—Edward Abbey, author

Man will occasionally stumble over the truth, but most of the time he will *pick himself up and continue on*.

—Winston Churchill, prime minister of Great Britain

It is always *your next move*.

—Napoleon Hill, author

There is no limit to what a man can do or where he can go if he doesn't mind who gets the credit.

—Motto on a plaque on Ronald Reagan's White House desk

One must from time to time attempt things that are beyond one's capacity.

—Pierre-Auguste Renoir, artist

Everyone who got where he is had to begin where he was.

—Robert Louis Stevenson, poet, author

It's a funny thing about life: *If you refuse to accept anything but the best, you very often get it.*

—W. Somerset Maugham, playwright

Don't be afraid to fail, but when you do, fail fast and laugh at yourself.

—Michael Houston, CEO of Grey North America

The *biggest mistake* a man in management can make is to *back down on a matter of principle*.

—Clarence Francis, chairman of General Foods

If the path were without risk, everyone would succeed.

—Michael Canic, president of Bridgeway Leadership, Vistage speaker

If we did all the things we are capable of doing, we would literally astonish ourselves.

—Thomas Edison, inventor

Once the game is over, the king and the pawn go back in the same box.

—Unknown

Experience tells you what to do; confidence allows you to do it.

—Stan Smith, professional tennis player

If you're too busy to learn, you won't be busy for very long.

—Unknown

If you do not develop a strategy on your own, you become part of someone else's strategy.

—Alvin Toffler, author

The trophies on one's shelf do *not win tomorrow's game.*

—Buck Rodgers, VP of marketing of IBM

Life begins at the edge of your comfort zone.

—Neale Donald Walsch, author

There are *few sorrows*, however poignant, in which **a good income is of no avail.**

—Logan Piersall Smith, author

If we can, why wouldn't we?

—Unknown

You are not required to *set yourself on fire just to* **keep other people warm.**

—Unknown

The secret of a successful organization is to get ordinary people to do extraordinary things.

—Peter Schutz, president and CEO of Porsche, Vistage speaker

If you ain't first, you're last.

—Ricky Bobby, character in the film *Talladega Nights*

CHAPTER 8

LET'S GET SERIOUS ABOUT HUMOR

Humor, appropriately applied in the workplace, can mean bigger deposits at the bank. Work should be fun.

To paraphrase, "There's no having fun in business." But of course there is, and done properly, there can also be a message.

Nationally known speaker-trainer Deanna Berg jested early in my career that perhaps a good motto for one of my CEOs would be "Wait for me. I'm your leader." His initial reaction was a faint smile. Upon second thought, he had realized that she'd given him a message.

As Mary Poppins said, "A spoonful of sugar helps the medicine go down."

Likewise, the West Virginia folk saying that "You can't get the water to clear up until you get the pigs out of the creek" has a humorous tone, but also a message for anyone reluctant to pull the plug on a staffer who just doesn't fit, maybe isn't pulling their weight, or doesn't align with the company's values.

Want things to be better, the water to be clear? Get pigs out of the water, the terrorists off the payroll.

Properly applied in the workplace, *humor can mean bigger deposits at the bank.*

People are living *longer than ever before*, a phenomenon undoubtedly made necessary by the *thirty-year mortgage*.

—Doug Larson, newspaper columnist

People often tell me that motivation doesn't last, and I tell them that *bathing doesn't either*. That's why I recommend it daily.

—Zig Ziglar, motivational speaker, author

If you fall on your face, at least you're moving forward.

—Richard Branson,
founder of Virgin Group

When the word *assistant* appears twice in your title, you can't really think you're a senior official.

—Michael Shepherd, CEO of BancWest

Don't confuse being out of bed with being awake.

—John O'Leary, motivational speaker, Vistage speaker

Wherever I go, I have to take myself— and that spoils everything.

—Murray Banks, PhD, psychologist and speaker

I don't know what we're going to do without you—*but we're starting tomorrow.*

—Unknown

You may not realize it when it happens, but a *kick in the teeth may be the best thing in the world for you.*

—Walt Disney, founder of the Walt Disney Company and Disney World

Everything will be all right in the end. So, if it is not all right, then it is not yet the end.

—Unknown

—Richard Grimes, managing director of Grimes Finishings Ltd.

There are very few people I trust in this world, and *I'm not one of them.*

Ninety-five percent of people make up their own statistics.

—Unknown

I love *mankind*; it's *people* I can't stand.

—Charles Schulz, cartoonist and creator of *Peanuts*

Money may not buy happiness, but *I'd rather cry in a Jaguar than on a bus.*

—Francoise Sagan, playwright

Life is tough, but it's tougher when you're stupid.

—John Wayne, actor, filmmaker

Work is the greatest thing in the world, so we should always save some of it for tomorrow.

—Don Herold, humorist

You can fool some of the people all of the time, and that's enough to make a profit.

—Unknown

Orville Wright didn't have a *pilot's license.*

—Richard Tait, founder of Cranium and Golazo

If life were fair, Elvis would be alive and all the impersonators would be dead.

—Johnny Carson, host
of the Tonight Show

When you are arguing with a fool, make sure he is *not doing the same thing.*

—Unknown

It's not a wake-up call if you go back to sleep.

—Greg Gutfeld,
TV personality, author

Nobody has to be perfect until you *fall in love* with them.

—Donald Phin, president of HRSherpas, Vistage speaker

The nine most terrifying words in the English language are "I'm from the government and I'm here to help."

—Ronald Reagan, U.S. president

There are three kinds of men. The one that learns by reading. The few who learn by observation. And the rest of them have to pee on the electric fence for themselves.

—Will Rogers, humorist, actor

Thunder is good, thunder is impressive, but it's _lightning that does the work._

—Mark Twain, author

It always looks darkest just before it gets totally black.

—Charles Schulz, cartoonist and creator of *Peanuts*

Things are more like they are *now* than they have ever been.

—Gerald Ford, U.S. president

You don't have to be nice to people on the way up if you're not coming back down.

—Colonel Tom Parker, personal manager of Elvis Presley

The trouble with quotes on the internet is that it's difficult to determine whether or not they are genuine.

—Abraham Lincoln, U.S. president (just kidding! Author Unknown)

Whenever you've got business trouble, the best thing to do is to get a lawyer. Then you got more trouble, but at least you got a lawyer.

—Chico Marx, comedian, actor

The closest anyone ever comes to perfection is on a job application.

—Unknown

The way I see it, if you want a rainbow, you gotta put up with the rain.

—Dolly Parton, singer/songwriter

A lot of fellows nowadays have a BA, MD, or PhD. Unfortunately, they don't have a J.O.B.

—Antoine "Fats" Domino, entertainer

If you obey all the rules, you miss all the fun.

—Katherine Hepburn, actress

The higher you climb the flagpole, the more people see your rear end.

—Don Meredith, pro football player, sports commentator

A mission statement is defined as "a long, awkward sentence that demonstrates management's inability to think clearly." All good companies have one.

—Scott Adams, creator of *Dilbert*

If I had any humility, *I would be perfect.*

—Ted Turner, founder of CNN and Turner Broadcasting System

Politicians and diapers have one thing in common: they should be *changed regularly and for the same reason.*

—Unknown

211

Hard work never killed anybody, but why take a chance?

—Charlie McCarthy, Edgar Bergen's ventriloquist's dummy

My opinions may have changed, but not the fact that I am right.

—Ashleigh Brilliant, cartoonist

It doesn't matter *how many times* you *fail*. You only have to be *right* once, and then everyone can tell you that you are an *overnight success*.

—Mark Cuban, owner of the Dallas Mavericks

Procrastination is like a credit card; it's a lot of fun until you get the bill.

—Christopher Parker, actor

There's no reason to be the *richest man in the cemetery. You can't do any business from there.*

—Unknown

That's all, folks!

—Porky Pig, *Looney Tunes* cartoon character

215

ABOUT THE AUTHOR

Bud Carter won national recognition as a radio station news director in Kansas City before becoming a TV anchorman in Peoria, Illinois. There, he went on to manage a radio station and became editor-publisher of a political and business-oriented weekly newspaper. The paper won national news coverage for itself during the Nixon years. It was there that he borrowed Ben Franklin's concept of penny wisdom and featured a quotation relevant to the focus of the day on the front page of each issue.

He was recruited to become the first Vistage (then TEC, or The Executive Committee) group chairman in the Southeastern U.S. in 1986 and soon started noting salient snippets shared by the speakers appearing before his Atlanta-based groups. Promoted to help grow the organization in the Southeast, Carter "published" his first edition of a self-published work titled "Pithy Business Quotes" in 1989—so that new Vistage group chairmen would have business-oriented content for their members' meeting folders.

Since then, Carter and his groups have heard more than a thousand speaker presentations—and he has now published thirteen editions perpetuating the key points made in the speakers' pithy quotes. Bud has a couple degrees (Liberal Arts and Journalism) from the University of Missouri and serves on the *Reporter Newspaper's* board, as well as that of Vistage Florida and the Atlanta Braves 400 Fan Club, Major League Baseball's second largest. He previously served on the boards of Coles Business College at Kennesaw State University, publicly traded Columbia Property Trust, Wells REIT I, the Rockbridge Commercial Bank, DiversiTech Corporation, WaveBase 9, and Creative Storage Systems. For nine years, Carter handled TEC management responsibilities (in addition to chairing his own groups), and was responsible for TEC's growth in the Southeast.

Carter and his wife, Kay, reside in suburban Atlanta. Bud professes to five passions: baseball, the pursuit of the perfect barbecue, racquetball—a sport in which he strives to accomplish mediocrity, jazz, and the quest for still more pithy quotes.

Have a great business quote you'd like to share? Please send your favorite quote to Bud for his ever-growing collection! Submissions can be sent to budcarter@aol.com.